THE RIVER GODS HAVE NO NAMES

SAMIKSHA SHEKHAR

Made with ♥ on the Notion Press Platform
www.notionpress.com

To the ones who never needed an altar to be sacred

Contents

Contents

Preface

for years I mistook my throat for a shrine-
until the river told me to spit out the holy water.

This wasn't meant to become a collection. It started with half-lines written in the backs of notebooks, in the Notes app at 2 a.m., on days I felt too much or nothing at all for two years.

The title came first—*The River Gods Have No Names*—and everything else flowed after, even if most of these poems don't mention rivers at all. But I've come to realize they speak of the same things: of shifting emotions, of quiet power, of movement without destination, of things unnamed but deeply felt.

These poems are about memory, growing pains, anger, guilt, inheritance, love, loss, softness, and learning how to carry yourself gently through it all. If you find even a fragment of yourself here, I'm glad the current brought you to this place.

Thank you for reading.

I came to the bank with empty hands.
The river took them anyway.
What emerges now is what the water
decided to spare-
these half-drowned words,
these songs that cannot be sung dry.

Read them wet.

Read them with the river still clinging to each syllable.

And when you finish,

know this:

what the water leaves behind is never what it took.

About The Author

Samiksha Shekhar, a 15 year old poet in motion.
I try to give my soul a chance to sing with its poetry, and connect with
similar souls out there just waiting to be heard.
There's not much going on about me, I'm ordinary like everyone else,
but as we've known, ordinary has a charm of bringing out the best of our
ourselves. So here I am with a thousand words on my mind, ready for them
to flow to you through the river of my thoughts.

1. Skin Of The River

We used to race boats
before we learned nothing survives the current.
Before we knew
how paper tears when kissed too long by water,
how names blur
when the ink is too eager to leave.
how even the neatest folds
can't keep a boat from sinking,
how something so light
can still drown.
We knelt by the stream,
palms wet with wonder,
mouths full of sky.
You said, *"Maybe the river is a mother,"*
and I believed you—
until she swallowed everything we gave her.

2. The Mythology Of My Mother's Hands

My mother's hands are not hands.
They are the first light breaking
over a field of rice,
the way it bends the stalks
into something like prayer.
I'd think they were made of water,
the way they could hold everything
without breaking.
I watch her peel an apple,
the skin falling in one long spiral,
and i think, *This is how the world begins-*
not with a bang, but with my mother's hands
turning the ordinary into something holy.
The lamp flickers above her,
and i think, *This is how stars are born-*
not from fire, but from the patience
of a woman who knows how to mend.
They say the gods live in the sky,
but i have seen them in her palms-
the way they cradled the weight of a thousand storms
and still found the strength to hold me.
I have seen them in the way she brushed my hair,
her fingers weaving through the tangles
smoothly like the words I didn't know yet how to say.

Now, when i look at my own hands
I see hers-
the way they shake when i'm tired,
the way they clench when i'm afraid.
She is the myth i carry,
the strength i didn't know i had.
Someday, I will tell the world
about the woman who built it
with her two hands-
how she never asked for a thank you,
how she never stopped giving,
even when her hands were empty.

"*The broken bone / is the loudest singer.*"

-Ocean Vuong, from 'Notebook Fragments.'

3. This Is How The Bone Learns To Sing

This is how the bone learns to sing:

firstly, it should forget it is a cage.

It must crack, must *ache*,

Must feel the weight of its own wanting.

You see, the body is a cathedral

Built from what it could not carry

Those ribs curved like the hull of a ship,

Hold the ocean you thought would drown you.

You thought silence is an armour.

You wore it like a second skin, let it settle

into the hollows of your chest.

But the heart is a restless thing-

it hums even when you want it to stop.

You are the crack in the vase,

where the light peaks through,

you are the sound a tree makes

when it falls on the forest bed

and no one is there to hear it.

You are not the echo of someone else's song.

You are the voice that hums in the dark,

the fist unclenching into a wing.

Someday you'll rise,

not because you were told to,

but because the music inside you,

refused to stay buried.

This is how the bone learns to sing:

By remembering it was never meant to stay silent.

“There is no wound deeper than the one that comes wrapped in love.”

4. Gentle

Once,
you held me like a question—
hands trembling,
as if afraid of the answer.
I thought that was love.
The way you paused before touching me,
like the body was a door
you'd forgotten how to knock on.
You kissed my shoulder.
I flinched.
You laughed.
I swallowed it.
The silence, I mean.
You said,
"Hurt is just another kind of holding."
So I called the bruises
pet names.
Called the nights
"storms that passed."
Called you
safe.
But what is love
if not the art of renaming the damage
until it purrs?

You said,
"I would never be him."
And for a moment,
I almost believed
you were softer than the fists
that taught me to hide.
But then came
the after.
The not-quite-violence.
The hands that never hit,
but held too long.
The words that landed
just under the skin,
where no one could see.
I tried to write you gentle.
Tried to carve your name
into something holy.
But no.
You're a monster too.

"I have created the thing I wanted to love, but it does not love me back."

5. Muse

I shaped you from the spaces
where my words grew empty.
You were a shadow at first,
a name I traced in the dark
when I couldn't find my own.
I wrote you
with ink made from silence.
I drew you with a trembling hand
that didn't know where the lines began
and where they ended.
I made you soft,
so I could feel the weight of your absence
and call it company.
I wrapped you in the language of longing
and made you something to worship.
But when you finally arrived,
you were not the shape I imagined.
You were the gaps in my own voice,
the lines I couldn't finish,
the echo I never learned how to name.
And yet,
I kept writing you.
Because maybe, if I could write long enough,
you'd start to believe in me.
Or maybe, I just needed someone

to stay still long enough
so I could see how little of you
was ever mine.

"The roots of the present grow in the past."

6. Flesh Of The Orchard

The orchard holds its breath
beneath the weight of old stories,
roots tangled in memory,
stretching deep into the earth
where silence grows thick with years.
We reach for the fruit,
heavy with the names of those
who wore the same hands
and harvested what they could from this land—
but the taste is never sweet enough.
There is always something bitter
in the flesh of the orchard.
I wonder, sometimes,
if the trees remember
the hands that planted them—
the ones who never saw the harvest,
who only dreamed of the ripening.
Their roots twist beneath mine,
a knot of unspoken things
I will never be free from.
I bite into the fruit,
and for a moment,
I am both them and me,
tasting the years that came before,
feeling the weight of what was given

and taken.
The orchard stands as witness,
bearing the scars of those who came before,
its branches heavy with promises
we are still too young to keep.

"Sometimes I think I invented you."

— Ocean Vuong, from 'On Earth We're Briefly Gorgeous'

7. Play Date

No one warned us
some games outgrow the players—
keep playing anyway.
You taught me how to stay quiet
without being still.
How to vanish
with your name in my mouth.
We stitched afternoons
from air and shadows,
called them kingdoms.
Made thrones out of silence,
ruled without noise.
Sometimes I spoke aloud
just to prove you answered.
Sometimes you didn't.
They say I was always alone.
That the chairs never moved.
That there were no footprints
but mine.
They say I was alone.
That the floor held only one set of steps.
That the door never opened.
No one told us
some games don't end.
They just wait—

quietly,
like breath beneath the bed.
You taught me how to lie
still enough to disappear.
To name silence a hiding place.
To stay until staying
meant forgetting how to leave.
We built worlds
out of almosts—
almost real,
almost seen,
almost enough.
You always let me win.
Even when I didn't notice.
Even when I wasn't trying.
Some afternoons
we'd make swords from twigs,
and you'd teach me how to fight
without hitting anything.
Said:
the first rule of winning is knowing when to run.
So we ran.
Past the mango tree.
Past the clothesline heavy with mother's silence.
Past the dog that never barked,
even when we stole its name
for the kingdom made of silence and rules
you never explained twice.

One evening,
I saved a part of something for you—
a slice of light, a soft place to land—
and found it untouched.
Not forgotten,
just… never needed.
I asked where you'd gone.
They blinked.
Said,
Who?
And I remembered
how the games never needed two voices.
How the footsteps
always echoed back as mine.
How the shadow
never quite lined up
with anything I could hold.

8. First Sight

You were not light,
but the crack it made —
a thin line splitting the quiet,
soft as a bruise blooming beneath my ribs.
I caught the pulse
of your breath against the room,
a tremor in the glass —
fragile, like the hush before rain.
Our eyes met in the space
where the world loses its weight,
and I was a moth held still
by a sudden flame.
Words hovered,
unsaid,
like leaves trembling
in a cold wind I couldn't name.
what passed between us
was less than a touch,
more than a breath.

"*Even sweetness can wound when held too long.*"

9. Red On My Tongue

Red on my tongue —
like crushed cherries,
sweet, bruised,
and bleeding slowly into silence.
The words I want to say
fall like ripe fruit,
heavy,
but never reach your ears whole.
They rot a little in the dark
before they leave me —
pulp and pit,
a taste that lingers long
after the voice is gone.
I hold them like secrets
in the hollow of my mouth,
flesh soft and trembling —
too fragile to unwrap,
too bitter to swallow.
Each syllable a scarlet thread
tied tight around my throat,
pulling me backward,
anchoring me
to the places I should forget.
Still, the red does not fade—
it stains my breath,

it colors my silence,
and waits
to bleed again.

"Prayer is not always answered; sometimes it is a language we invent to keep ourselves speaking."

10. Petition In A Dead Language

They handed me grief
like scripture,
but no one stayed to translate it.
So I read it aloud anyway—
stumbling through
each unfamiliar syllable
as if pain had a grammar.
The sky listens
like a judge with no face.
And I,
just another voice
bleeding vowels
into a mouthless god.
I call it prayer
but it feels
like a voicemail
left on a number
no longer in service.
What is devotion
if the altar no longer answers?
What is language
if not an echo
of something already gone?

So I kneel—not to beg,
but to remember
how it feels
to believe
something is listening.

"Memory is the only paradise from which we cannot be expelled."

11. Silence

They say things will be easier someday—
words tucked behind silence,
wrapped in good intentions
that don't quite reach.
Sometimes the air feels heavy,
like a room that holds its breath,
waiting for a sound
that never comes.
There's love here,
but it's a quiet thing,
wearing a mask
that doesn't always fit.
You learn early
how to fold your hands
and soften your voice,
how to keep the storm
tucked behind your ribs—
a secret tide
no one sees rising.
The space between words
is where you live,
where meaning slips like water
through the cracks
and disappears before you catch it.

Lessons are given
in silence and glances—
how to stand small,
how to carry weight
without letting it show.
You gather your breath
like fragile glass,
knowing the smallest crack
could shatter everything.
They say you'll understand later,
when the world grows wider,
but sometimes understanding
is just knowing when to stay quiet,
when to let the silence
do the talking.
And maybe that's all love is—
a river that never breaks the surface,
carrying pieces
you learn not to hold.

"Faith that cannot bear questions is not faith. It's fear."

12. An Altar Where My Name Was Never Called

To question is not to betray. This poem is not against belief, only against the kind that refuses to be questioned, against the kind that asks you to kneel before you even understand why.

I lit every candle
with my mouth closed.
They told me silence
was a kind of offering.
I folded my hands
into the shape of a prayer
and forgot how to hold
anything else.
Guilt bloomed early—
not mine,
but passed down
like a name I never chose.
Every time I bowed,
I lost a piece of spine.
I mistook breaking
for reverence.
Once,
I whispered a question,

and the ceiling cracked.
So I learned to swallow
every doubt like dust.
Now,
I stand before a god
with my face wiped clean,
my voice erased,
and wonder—
what kind of worship
asks you to leave
yourself
outside the door?

"Not all decay smells. Some sits quietly inside you, turning everything to ash."

13. Corrosion Begins At The Heart

The guilt didn't come all at once.
It gathered,
like water in a place I forgot to dry.
First, a stain.
Then, the slow red of rust
blooming through the metal.
I kept the lie small,
tucked beneath the tongue
like a coin swallowed in childhood—
thinking the body
would forget what the mouth refused to say.
But even steel learns softness
under enough rain.
I said nothing.
Again and again.
And the silence grew teeth.
You touched my shoulder,
called it love.
But by then,
I had already left fingerprints
on things I could not clean.
Somewhere between
truth and keeping peace,
I let the acid in.

I've stopped raising my voice—
not out of peace,
but because rust gathers quickest
in places
you pretend are clean.
And I am tired
of polishing pain
for forgiveness.

"*There are no words for the silence between us.*"

14. Nothing Is New

I never learned to ask
about the spaces between things,
how light falls uneven,
how shadows hold secrets
they'll never tell.
We used to watch the clock,
but time slipped
in corners we never touched.
The air was always
a little too thick
for easy conversation.
I don't know why
the floor creaked in certain places,
why the windows seemed to watch
instead of open.
But we never asked.
We just knew the rhythm
of being still.
In the garden,
the flowers bloomed in order,
but I never understood
the way they bent under the weight
of something quiet.
There was always something left unsaid—
not a word,

but a space
we were too polite to fill.
But I'm fine,
I know how to carry myself
around rooms like these,
where the light is always
just a little off-center.

"The river will carry you, but it will never tell you where it is going."

— Rick Riordan, from 'The Blood of Olympus'

15. Drowning

The water doesn't rise.
You simply stop holding the boat.
First go the fingers—
stiff from cradling a thing
that was never meant to stay.
Then the words,
floating like ink on wet paper,
sinking,
slipping away like a name lost downstream.
Then the voice,
soft as ink bleeding through
the boat's spine.
Grief wears the face
of someone who gently lowers you
into yourself.
This is not drowning.
This is forgetting to surface-
Just as she swallowed everything we gave her,
and still asked for *more*.

"*Existence is neither answer nor question. It is simply the quiet moment between breaths,
the space where everything else folds away,
and all that remains is being.*"

16. Subject: Existence

Subject: Existence
To: Whoever cares to read

Hi,

I'm here — not perfect, not broken, just somewhere in between.

I laugh loud enough to forget the small stuff,

but sometimes I still trip over it.

I've attached a few things —

a bruise from running into life too fast,

a smile I wore just yesterday,

and a reminder that I'm still figuring it out.

Time doesn't always behave —

some days it's a sprint, some days it drags like Monday morning.

And the light? It flickers sometimes —

maybe it's nervous too.

I don't need big answers, just a nod that existence is okay.

That being here, with the mess and the joy,

is enough.

So here I am, trying to not take things too deeply,

still learning to celebrate the little wins.

Attachments:

-a laugh from last weekend

-a half-remembered dream

-proof that showing up is enough

No need to reply — unless you want to.

Regards.

Acknowledgement

"some gods refuse to be carved into stone."

Thank you to whoever who decided to give their time to read this.

I would like to thank the following authors for their work that shaped and inspired the poems in this collection, quoting some of their lines as the epigraphs-

- Arundhati Roy, 'The God of Small Things' (1997)
- Nayyirah Waheed, 'Salt' (2013)
- Ocean Vuong, 'Notebook Fragments' (2017)
- Ocean Vuong, 'On Earth We're Briefly Gorgeous' (2019)
- Rick Riordan, 'The Blood of Olympus' (2014)
- Ray Bradbury, 'Fahrenheit 451' (1953)

I would like to thank a few people, in no special order <3

To my elder brother,

Shaurya Shekhar, you've always been the person I've looked up to the most (annoying, I know). I genuinely can't imagine a world where we weren't siblings—some cosmic glitch would've had to fix it. Thank you for being the best brother ever. Even though we're complete opposites in what we like, you still somehow get me better than most people do.

ACKNOWLEDGEMENT

To my parents,

My father, Sanjay Shekhar and my mother Shalini Shekhar. Thank you for always encouraging me, even when this didn't look like the most practical path. For giving me the space to explore, create, and try things on my own terms. Your support means more than I say- after all we do know my words on paper contrast better than the words from my tongue- Thank you for being amazing parents.

To my grandparents,

Especially my maternal grandfather where I probably get my writing skills from, Professor B.N. Jha, who has written several books in his own fielf of chemistry as well as spirituality. Equally so, my other family members and grandparents have surely been good influences and constants in my life.

To my friends,

For reading the messy drafts, for encouraging me, and for standing beside me even when the metaphors and trials of our young lives got too heavy.

To my reading communities and school book club,

For making stories a shared joy and giving me a safe space. You reminded me that loving books is never a lonely thing.

To the books and authors that made me fall in love with words,

Thank you for teaching me that language is both wound and balm. Your words helped me find mine.

Finally, to my future self,

I hope you're still writing. I hope you're still soft in the ways that matter, even if the world tried to harden you. And if things feel heavy—just remember, this was proof you once believed in yourself enough to begin.

For whoever who needed this, I hope it found you,
- Samiksha Shekhar

"*I think I must have been made of water in another life, but I never learned to swim.*"

— *Ray Bradbury, from 'Fahrenheit 451'*